young, gay & proud!

"Those of us who agonized through our coming out, who *knew* we were the only person in the world to ever feel this way, can be justifiably jealous of the kids who will never have to experience those things because they found this book."

Sarajean Garten, in **The Advocate**

"The best introduction to gay life for young people yet, offering clear advice on coming out to parents, dealing with friends and peers and the fear of their rejection, meeting other gays, health issues and gay sexuality."

Stephen MacDonald, in **Emergency Librarian**

D1337657

Cover design and all illustrations by Beth Ireland

young, gay & proud!

Alyson Publications, Inc. • Boston, Massachusetts

Much of this book was originally published in Australia, under the same title, by the Gay Teachers and Students Group of Melbourne. This U.S. edition of **Young, Gay and Proud** was prepared by Sasha Alyson with the help and cooperation of Enid Braun, Beth Ireland, and writers who have individually signed their work.

Text of U.S. edition copyright © 1980, 1981 by Alyson Publications Inc.
All illustrations copyright © 1980 by Beth Ireland

Typeset by Larry Goldbaum
Manufactured entirely in the United States of America.

First edition, second printing: August 1981

ISBN 0 932870 01 5

Contents

Introduction

If you're a girl you might find that most of the other girls have got crushes on Starsky and Hutch, but you wouldn't miss an episode of the Bionic Woman.

If you're a boy you might go to the football game to watch all those hunky guys playing, and if your team wins, that's O.K. too.

Maybe most of the other kids are "growing out of" the hero-worship they've had for some teacher or kid of the same sex, but you know you're not worshipping heroes — it's just that you feel really great about those people and that's all that matters.

Maybe you feel embarrassed when your friends give you a hard time about not showing much interest in the opposite sex and you feel a bit scared about telling them who you're really interested in.

Maybe you aren't sure who you're interested in. You don't particularly enjoy regular dating, but you aren't really sure that you're gay, either.

Well, you're the sort of person this book is written for. It was written by lesbians and gay men who have gone through many of the same experiences that you have. We've felt many of the same pains and joys that come from being young and gay. We're sick of the fact that books used in school always assume that all young people are straight. We wrote this one to start to even things up.

That's going to be hard because a lot of things need changing first. For instance, schools have to change before things are evened up. Most of them aren't such great places to spend all day in, especially for students — or teachers — who are gay.

Not so long ago, nobody talked about homosexuals in schools at all. Now some people do, but they've mostly got it all wrong. They talk about homosexuality like they talk about measles, like it's some sort of disease. It's up to us, all of us, to get the story right. That means being strong enough to say "Yes, I'm gay," or "Yes, I'm a lesbian," or "Yes, I'm a faggot."

That might sound hard now but by the time you've finished reading this book we hope you'll feel a lot stronger. You'll know that being gay is O.K., you're not alone, and together we can start to put things right.

Are these some of the questions on your mind? If so, then this book is for you.

• I get turned on by other guys. Does that mean I'm a fairy? P.S. I don't look like one.

• My best friend says she's a lesbian. Should I drop her before she tries anything on me?

B.IRELAND

• I know my teacher's gay —
I saw her at a gay dance.
Should I let her know that I
know? (She's really nice.)

• I don't know what I am.
Sometimes women turn me
on, sometimes guys. Does
that mean I'm bi? If so,
should I forget about
marriage?

• The gays I know aren't the
sort of people I like or want
to have anything to do with.
Where do I meet guys like
me?

• I've heard about treatment
for being queer. Does it
work?

• I'm gay now — but I've got
a girlfriend. Will I grow out
of it if I get married?

• I'm in love with a friend —
but she's straight. I want to
tell her about me but I'm
scared she'll freak. What
should I do?

• Do gay couples stay
together like married ones?
I'm scared of growing old
all alone.

• I always thought I'd grow
out of liking guys. But I
know now that I'm not going
to. What should I do?

• I'm gay, 16 years old, and
I'm in love with a guy ten
years older than me. If we
have sex and my parents find
out, what can happen to me?
Would he go to jail?

• I think I'm straight — but
sometimes I think about how
it would be to be with a
woman. Is that normal?

• How do you pick a lesbian
from a straight girl? Gee it's
certainly hard. I always end
up picking the straight ones.
Stupid, isn't it?

Getting started

B.IRELAND

Some people have their first gay feelings when they're children, some when they're much older. But it seems most people begin to consciously notice their gay feelings at puberty. This usually happens sometime between the age of 10 and 15 years, a bit later for boys than for girls.

You notice in a movie that you get turned on by someone of the same sex. Or at school you can't keep your mind off a friend or a teacher of the same sex as you. You find it pleasant to just look at them. When you're away from them you enjoy thinking about them, and you may imagine them in all sorts of sexy ways. You might even get turned on by them in your dreams.

Only you know how strong your feelings are and what they mean to you. Some people will tell you that you're too young to know your mind. They'll say that your gay feelings will go away as you get older. That might be true for some people, but so what! For gay people they do *not* go away. This is just one of the ways that ignorant people try to talk us out of being who we really are. No one would ever dream of telling heterosexual kids that they might be on the wrong track.

Young people however *are* often told to wait until they are older, or until they get married, before they have sex. At least this is what many adults say. In fact most adults think it's OK if boys have sex while they're in high school. But girls are expected to follow different standards. Boys are likely to be called virile for having frequent sex. Girls are likely to be called sluts.

These rules obviously don't make sense — especially if you're a girl. In fact most of the old ideas of what's right or wrong about sex don't make sense. There are all sorts of stupid rules, like nobody was supposed to talk about sex or enjoy it — especially women. Church teaching has had a lot to do with this, just as the church has had a lot to do with the laws and customs that made things so hard for gays.

No one has the right to make people feel bad about their sexual choice. Sex by itself does not harm anyone. What really does harm people are the deliberate lies that are so often spread about sex. For instance being told that sex is dirty, or that sex is only for marriage. These sorts of ideas really do screw people up.

On the opposite extreme, some people will say that if you *don't* have sex, there's something wrong with you. They have no more business trying to run your life than the first group does.

The one rule we need is simple: do what seems right to you, and take care not to hurt anyone else.

You're not the only one

BIRELAND

Shere Hite, in her 1976 *Hite Report* on female sexuality, found that about 8% of all women thought of themselves as lesbians. Another 9% had had sexual relationships with both men and women.

For males, we have figures from Alfred Kinsey, a famous sex researcher. He found that out of every 100 American adult men, 37% had had at least one gay sexual experience, 10% liked their own sex best, and 4% were gay for their whole lives.

These numbers are likely to be a bit on the low side, since some people won't admit they've had gay experiences.

These figures show us three things:

1. A lot of people who are mainly straight have gay feelings and gay sex from time to time.
2. About 10% of the adult population (men and women) are gay.
3. Some people change around

a bit. Sometimes they feel straight, sometimes they feel gay.

Practically all researchers agree that a person's sexual preference is determined early in life. That means that in high school, like in adult life, roughly one person in ten is going to have strong gay feelings. Many of them won't realize yet that they are gay — the pressures to fit the heterosexual norm are strong. And some will know it, but hide it. But if you're feeling lonely, it helps to remember that you have lots of gay classmates.

You might be wondering where bisexuals fit into all this. And that's a good question. It all depends on what you mean by bisexual.

A true bisexual is someone who doesn't have a clear-cut preference. There *are* people like this around — but we don't know how many. What you're more likely to meet are people who say they're bisexual, when in fact they're really gay. They make out they're bisexual because they know the rest of the world says that being bisexual is not as bad as being gay. If you say you're bisexual then people who are hung-up about homosexuality can switch on to the straight bit of you, and forget about the gay part. Which of course is a real put down of us.

Some people who are basically straight, but occasionally "swing the other way" call themselves "bi." This book is not written specially for them, but we hope they might enjoy reading the parts that apply.

Where are we all?

The people we *know* to be gay are just the top of the ice-berg. You can't always pick gay people from the way we look. Most of us look pretty ordinary, and some of us are in good disguise. For instance many are married. According to one estimate, about one in three of all lesbians are married, and many of them are mothers.

We're spread across all social classes too. From movie stars to the Communist Party, from New York City to Dubuque, Iowa, from construction workers to the woman next door . . . we're everywhere.

If there are 50 teachers in your school, the chances are that about 5 of them will be gay. And about 18 of them will have had some gay sexual experience. If there are 30 kids in your class, three of them will like their own sex best.

Only a few gay teachers have let the world know they're gay.

The reason is that if they did, many wouldn't have a job. Because we are so hard to pick out one of our biggest problems is meeting each other. There are places where gays meet — clubs, groups, etc. — and the gay phone services can tell you about these.

Telling people we're gay, starting with a few friends we can trust, is another good way of meeting other gays. If they're not gay themselves they often know someone who is. You'll be surprised how many of the people who are shocked when they first hear that you're gay are telling you, five minutes later, about a gay friend they want to introduce you to.

When we're all free to be ourselves, open and proud of our way of loving, only then will the straight world see that gay people come in all shapes and sizes . . . and we really are *everywhere*.

Letters

Dear Friends,

I am 16 years old and I don't know where my head is at now. I have never had a boyfriend and have no desire to have one. I have never made love with a boy and I now believe I am a homosexual.

I have a female friend whom I like very much but am very reluctant and too shy to approach her. I really need help.

I hope you do not think that this is some kind of crank writing to you as a joke as I am very serious and I need help with this matter.

        Country Girl.

Dear Country Girl,

Obviously no one else can tell you whether you are homosexual, bisexual, or whatever; this is something you must work out for yourself. If you do come to feel you are homosexual or bisexual you would probably find it helpful and supportive to meet other homosexual women. This may be more difficult in your case because you live in the country, and most of the homosexual bars and groups are in the city. Of course there are many homosexuals living in the country, but most of them are reluctant to "come out" and organize activities in their own towns because of the likelihood of gossip and discrimination against them.

You mention that you have a female friend whom you like very much but you are shy about approaching her. Since I don't know you or your friend I cant tell you what you should do. However, I know a number of women who have been in the same position so it might help if I list the possibilities as I see them.

(a) You might approach your friend and find that she feels the same way, and this might result in a happy and successful relationship.

(b) You might begin a

B.IRELAND

relationship and then your friend might decide that she prefers men, or that she feels too guilty, or that she wants the security of marriage — heterosexual affairs also break up from time to time, but there is a lot more pressure from outside on homosexual ones.

(c) You might want to tell your friend that you think you're a lesbian, but not say that you are attracted to her until you know more about her feelings. Just being able to talk about your gay feelings with a friend is helpful.

(d) Your friend might say that she does not want a sexual relationship with you but that she wants to keep friendship as before.

(e) She might break off the friendship altogether.

(f) She might feel so upset that she not only breaks off the friendship but also complains about you to her family or yours or your friends.

(g) You might remain silent and unhappy.

You will have to weigh up these possibilities in the light of your knowledge of your friend and of your own feelings.

Good luck. I hope you will write again and tell me how you are getting along.

Dear Friends,

I'm a 16 year old male, and for years now I've wondered if I'm completely normal. I get turned on by girls sometimes — not to look at, just when we kiss and muck around. It's different with guys though. Often I'll get a hard-on even thinking about a good looking guy. When I go into the showers after gym it really gets me going. I have to cover up quick before they all notice.

Now you might think that I look like a queer. Well I don't. I would have no worries getting a steady girl. Do you think if I keep going out with girls things will work out?

I wouldn't mind meeting a guy who is like me and looks normal. I'm not interested in pansy types.

I don't know if I'm hetero, homo or bi. I think about this a lot. I know I need help.
Rick.

Dear Rick,

It sounds like you do have stronger feelings for guys, and going out with girls is not likely to change that. You have homosexual feelings, and you should accept them as normal. You may be homosexual or you may be bisexual. That's something you'll have to work out.

If you go out with a girl it should be because you are attracted to her, and not because you are scared of being homosexual, or want to appear manly. You really can't tell homosexuals by the way they look unless they want you to know.

If you go to gay meeting spots you will find many men like yourself. But why are you so worried about appearance? It's hard in this society for anyone who looks like a homosexual. People who don't hide what they are ought to be admired for their courage, even if they are not the type who attract you. Have you ever thought what they have to put up with in the way of bashings and insulting remarks? They have a lot more guts than some of the manly types.

You might be interested to read the story of a football player who came out as gay in 1975 — *The David Kopay Story*. He writes about how he came to change his idea of what's manly in coming to accept his homosexuality.

Dear Friends,

I'm gay, I'm 17 years old and my name is Maria.

I thought it time I should ask someone for advice on how to speak my mind to friends about my being gay. At least they were friends before they found out.

They have called me sick, queer, etc., two of them even said they pity me. I think that is sad and funny. Sad because they say I've lost control over my feelings for girls (one in particular), sad 'cause I'm being forced to resent my feelings. I'm getting sick of thinking before speaking, and trying not to look at her when we are out at a public place. I am very careless nowadays because with every passing day I love her just so much more and this feeling seems so natural.

On the other hand it is funny because they think I am the one to be pitied. I think that is really funny, so funny I could cry. I'm not ashamed of what I am and who I mix with. I pity them, the ones that call themselves 'straight' (which is a lot of shit) for missing out on something beautiful.

Maria.

Dear Maria,

I don't think you need my advice about how to handle your straight friends. You are doing a great job now. But perhaps you need to meet more gay people and get their support.

I agree that your friends are the ones who are behaving strangely, and not you. People are often very uptight and confused about sex in general and homosexuality in particular, but pretend to know all about it. However nasty people are, it's often a weight off your mind to tell people you are gay. Then you don't have to worry about them finding out somehow and you feel more respect for yourself because you've been honest and straightforward.

Getting to know people

by Scott Calvin

Ever since I can remember, I've been attracted to males in a sort of mysterious way that I didn't understand. I remember, in sixth grade, seeing a picture of Michelangelo's statue of David, and being very excited by it. I've spent hours since then looking through books of Greek and Renaissance sculpture! I didn't think of it as a sexual thing, though I knew I shouldn't let anybody catch me doing it. I just liked to look.

In eighth grade, I had a close friend who lived a few blocks away. We did everything together, and when we were apart I spent most of my time thinking about him. Now I realize I had a crush on him, but I never thought about it like that at the time. We were just great friends.

In ninth grade, he suddenly started having nothing to do with me. He didn't explain anything, he just ignored me. I was so hurt that I didn't know what to do. I guess he understood me better than I understood myself, and he was afraid people might start saying things.

Part of me must have known I was homosexual then, and part of me didn't. Every time I saw a book that had anything to do with sex, I'd pick it up and check the index to see what it said about homosexuality. Obviously I knew that had something to do with me! But I never consciously thought of myself as gay.

Last year, that changed. I was visiting my friend Mark who lives in Milwaukee (I live in a suburb nearby). I knew Mark was gay and it didn't bother me and I knew I liked him a lot. Well, I guess I was attracted to him, too! We were very close, and one evening when we ended up making love, it was very exciting but it also seemed like a perfectly natural thing to do. Mark gave me a lot of encouragement to think about homosexuality, and finally I was able to say to myself, "Yes, I'm gay."

A month or two later, I mentioned to Mark that I'd like to meet other gay people, because he was the only one I knew. So we went to one of the gay bars and Mark introduced me to some of his friends. Pretty soon a man came over and bought me a drink, and we talked for a while. He was quite likable. I mentioned that I liked classical music, and he asked if I'd like to come over to his

B. Ieveno

apartment and listen to records. Sure, I said, and we went.

Well, to make a long story short, I was incredibly naive. He was mainly interested in sex, and I just wanted to listen to records, so it was not a real comfortable evening.

I almost didn't want to go back to the bar any more after that, but Mark convinced me to go again with him. I'm glad he did.

I've learned now to avoid situations like that. If I like somebody but I'm not interested in them sexually, I have the sense not to "go over to their apartment to listen to music" unless I'm sure that's all they want. If somebody approaches me in a bar and I really don't like him, I can politely discourage him. Twice I've even gotten up the nerve to walk up to somebody I didn't know and ask them to dance! (Both times they said yes, thank God!)

So one or two week-ends a month I go into the city and now I feel at home in the bar. I'm with people like me, and many of them I know, at least slightly. Some are good friends by now. And I don't have to *pretend* anything! It's a wonderful change from school.

My advice for other gay young people is, if you're feeling isolated and alone, try to get out where there are other gays. Bars, or discos, or social clubs, or gay liberation groups, or work for a gay newspaper, or whatever. Maybe, like me, you'll feel a little intimidated by some of these places at first (it's easier if you go with a friend), but after a while you won't know how you survived without them.

Big lies & funny pictures

We've all been around people talking about faggots and dykes and making jokes about them. Often these people pretend to act gay. When they make jokes about faggots they flap their wrists, talk in a high voice and walk around wiggling their bums. To them this is how every gay man is supposed to look and act.

When a dyke is being made fun of she is always talked about as being big with short hair and a deep voice, wearing rough clothes and acting tough. This is what every lesbian is supposed to look like.

The jokes make us look weird and stupid, and if we're around when this goes on we don't feel too good either.

How true are these pictures?

About one in every ten people in the population is gay. Does one in every ten people look like the joke picture of a gay woman or man to you? Obviously not. Most times you can't pick gay people unless they want you to know.

A few gay men act in a feminine way (like a woman), and a few gay women act in a masculine way (like a man) just for the fun of it. This is their way of challenging the straight world. For others, this way of life is natural and they're just being themselves. Some straight men act in a feminine way too. And they get trashed. Those people who are like the joke pictures of gays — whether they're straight or gay — get the trashing that's meant for all gay people.

As well as these pictures there are a lot of other wild stories and lies flying around about us. Here are a few examples.

1. GAY COUPLES DON'T STICK TOGETHER FOR VERY LONG.
FACT: *Even though there are a*

lot of mean and stupid hassles put on us by the straight world to try and break us up, lots of us have loving and long-lasting relationships. But then again some of us simply aren't interested in having long relationships or being in a twosome forever. This is the same now for more and more straight people too.

2. WOMEN BECOME GAY BECAUSE THEY CAN'T GET A MAN. IT'S THE SECOND BEST THING.
FACT: *This is another lie spread around by straight men who can't live with the truth that there are some women who just aren't interested in them. For a lesbian, being with other women is the only choice they ever want to make. Some women, even after years of marriage, find that they really prefer other women and become lesbians.*

3. GAY WOMEN HATE MEN AND ARE FRIGHTENED OF THEM.
FACT: *Because of the rotten way that women are treated in this society, there is plenty of reason for women to feel angry*

towards men. Why should gay women feel any different? But to say that lesbians are frightened of men is silly. The truth is that gay women find that their emotional and physical and sexual needs are best filled by other women.*

4. GAY WOMEN AND MEN WANT TO SLEEP WITH EVERY STRAIGHT PERSON THEY SEE.
FACT: *Gays don't want to get off with anyone who is not interested, whether they are straight or gay. There is nothing wrong with letting someone know that you are attracted to them, but we should all be prepared to take no for an answer. Anyway, why should straight people be so vain to think that we would all be attracted to them!*

5. GAY MEN ARE FRIGHTENED OF WOMEN AND HATE ALL WOMEN.
FACT: *Most gay men don't hate women at all, it's just that they prefer to choose other men to be close to. In fact lots of gay men have women as their best friends. Some gay men, after years of marriage, find that*

they really prefer other men and become homosexuals.

6. GAY PEOPLE WANT TO TURN AS MANY PEOPLE AS THEY CAN INTO DYKES AND FAGGOTS.

FACT: *The straight world has been trying to turn us into straights by using every method under the sun, including torture, and it has never worked. You just can't force a straight person to be gay, just as you can't force a gay person to be straight. If a straight person gets off with a gay person it is because they both wanted it to happen.*

7. GAY PEOPLE LEAD SAD, LONELY LIVES.

FACT: *Some heavy straight people seem to spend an awful lot of time and effort trying to make us unhappy and bored. But now that gay people are starting to fight back and getting to like each other more and more, these hassles are just not working. As we grow older, even if we don't have lovers, we*

B.IRELAND

usually have a group of close friends we can count on and who can count on us.

8. HOMOSEXUALITY IS UNNATURAL
FACT: *There's nothing unnatural about loving or being attracted to someone of the same sex. Homosexuality is known to have existed in some form in almost all human cultures. In many cultures, it has been accepted and even encouraged.*

Lesbian and homosexual behavior has also been widely observed in many mammals including cows, horses, sheep, pigs, rabbits, hamsters, and chimpanzees. Even porcupines

— but don't ask us how they do it.

All these myths are made up to convince people that being straight is best, and that the way of life of the straight world is the only one possible. These stories are also spread about with the idea that we will want to hide away and keep quiet about ourselves.

Sometimes life is made hard for us, not because we are gay in the first place, but because so many people believe the lies about us. The last thing we should do is start believing these stories ourselves.

Self-images

Having a good self-image is important for any human being. Growing up gay, achieving that can be hard, because practically every gay person you'll see in movies or on TV, or read about in novels, is shown in a very negative way.

Many people, for example, get their first impression of gay life from the book *Everything You Always Wanted to Know About Sex, But were Afraid to Ask*. The author of that book seems to have decided that the fastest way to make a buck was to make gays the butt of his jokes. He presents an unusually bigoted view of gay people and gay lifestyles. Unfortunately, that's all that many people have to go on.

There *are* books that will help you feel happy about being gay; books that will help you develop a sense of identity as a gay person. Novels can be especially good for this, and you'll find lots of suggestions at the back of this book.

Some novels with strong lesbian characters that you're likely to enjoy are *Happy Endings are All Alike* by Sandra Scoppettone, *Yesterday's Lessons* by Sharon Isabelle, and *The Young in One Another's Arms* by Jane Rule. And don't forget *Rubyfruit Jungle*, by Rita Mae Brown.

For novels with gay male characters we'd recommend many of Mary Renault's books (especially *The Charioteer* and *The Persian Boy*), *The City and the Pillar* by Gore Vidal, *The Front Runner* by Patricia Nell Warren, and *Maurice*, by E.M. Forster.

Why are we hassled?

As gay people, we are hassled by lots of Big Lies being spread about us. A lot of people go on believing them. And not enough of the people who don't believe the lies speak up.

Why do they believe the lies? Well, because they're often spread by ministers, doctors, politicians, judges, and newspapers, even teachers — and the man or woman on the street expects those sorts of people to know what they're talking about. Besides, it's easier — and safer — to believe what you're told rather than to think for yourself and ask tricky questions.

There have always been people who could see through the lies — but usually they kept silent because they were lazy, or scared, or had no say in things... or a bit of each. Up till recently you weren't listened to if you spoke up about homosexuality unless you were a minister or doctor or lawmaker.

Then gay people started putting the record right. This started happening in the late 1960's. Since then there has been a lot more disagreement among ministers and doctors. And among ourselves too.

You might wonder why the lies got invented in the first place, and why they've hung around for so long. No one knows the exact answer to this, but here are some ideas.

WE'RE DIFFERENT?

Some people say that gays get hassled because we're different. People are often scared of what they don't understand. This is so for other people, like immigrants. It's happened to Jews a lot, and it even used to happen to left-handers. Did you know that people used to believe that left-handers were possessed by the devil? When things went wrong, the left-handers got the blame. And society tried to make them into right-handers. Sound familiar?

THE CHURCH?

Another reason is the way our society treats sex. Most of the straight world's ideas about sex can be traced back to church teaching, and the Christian church has always been freaked out by sex. Around 700 B.C. the Hebrew church set up laws which made 36 crimes punishable by death, and half of these were to do with sex. The penalty for males guilty of homosexual acts was death by stoning, the most severe penalty. There were no laws against lesbianism. Women's sexuality wasn't taken seriously then, either.

For centuries now the church has said that sex is only OK between married people so that they can have children. If people enjoy sex in any other way — by themselves, with someone of the same sex, or with someone they're not married to — then the church calls them *sinners* and tries to make them feel bad. Like the feeling you have if your parents catch you masturbating?

PSYCHIATRISTS?

Where the church is losing its grip, as it seems to be in our society, you'd think we'd be better off. But it doesn't work that way. The reason is that psychiatrists (shrinks) are doing much the same job as the church. Shrinks are special doctors who tell people the right and wrong way to behave. When they don't like the way you are, they say you are sick, just like the Church tells people they are sinners. Some people say that shrinks are a bit like the witch doctors of the olden days. They charge a lot of money just to make you worry.

It's no wonder then that so many people today are screwed up about sex. If they haven't actually broken the church's and shrink's rules, then they feel bad about wanting to!

Kinsey's figures show that lots of people have homosexual feelings, not just people like us who call ourselves gay. People who don't like to face up to those feelings may be especially nasty towards gay people.

When people try and keep things pushed down, something might snap, and they will do some very violent things. If gay people can be picked out, we may become the target of this violence.

One of the main reasons we get picked on is because such a big deal is made about *men making it with women*. This is supposed to be *the* way of proving how much of a man or how much of a woman you are.

Men are supposed to act tough, get married and boss their wives around. Women are supposed to be weak, a bit stupid, and need men to lean on.

Anyone who doesn't go along with these ideas, even if they're *not* gay, often still gets called a dyke or fairy.

Any boy who doesn't want to play football or other rough games will often get called a sissy or a fairy.

Any girl who is good at sport gets called *tough* or a dyke and the other girls tell her that the boys won't like her if she's too good at sport. Girls are made to feel bad about anything they are good at unless it's sewing or cooking.

A woman who demands a better deal often gets called a *dyke*.

A man who's gentle often gets called a *fairy*.

You can see that the words *dyke* and *fairy* are used to make everyone toe the line!

Lesbians: getting stepped on twice

Lesbians are always going to get hassled two ways as long as our society is being run the way it is now.

First, lesbians get put down because of being women. Being a woman means not getting a fair chance most of the time. There are lots of things women and girls aren't allowed to do just because of being female. You probably know some yourself.

In some schools, girls aren't allowed to play sports like football in P.E. classes, let alone take part in competitive sports.

Maybe you're in a school that encourages you to take home economics or typing instead of woodworking or metal work or something else only the boys are expected to do. Maybe some of the boys don't want to do woodworking but they don't get any choice either.

When you leave school you'll find that there are a lot of jobs that we don't get an equal chance at, like being a train conductor, or even an auto mechanic.

You might think things have gotten better since Women's Liberation groups really got started about ten years ago. Some important things like equal pay have been won for some women, but even such a basic thing like that hasn't been won for all women. There are still a lot of things that need to be changed. One example is the abortion laws. Abortions are legal now but Congress has stopped public funding (Medicaid) for women who can't afford to pay for abortions.

Most men don't want things to change. Men have got power over women, and because they have more opportunities than women they think that when women start fighting *they* are going to be the losers. They'd rather keep things the way they are now.

There are also some very powerful men making stacks of money out of keeping women down. Because it is hard for women to get jobs they can make them work in rotten jobs for low pay and long hours. You don't have to look very hard to see that women get the worst jobs (if they get a job at all) and are first to be fired whenever it suits the boss.

As well as being put down for being women, lesbians get put down for being gay. Most men are scared of lesbians.

Lesbians aren't doing what men want them to do. They're not closed up in a house cooking, washing and ironing for men and the family. Lesbians are not dependent on men for money, or to provide them with somewhere to live, like a lot of married women are.

At the same time, lesbians have to support themselves on the salaries they get as single women. This is hard sometimes because although men are supposed to be paid salaries that will help support a family, women are only paid salaries as if they are adding to a husband's income. If you're not married, you will have less to

live on than a man would. Also, some lesbians are mothers, and it is especially hard for single mothers to support children on a woman's salary.

So we've got two major things to fight: being put down as women, and being put down for being gay.

So what do we do about it?

Well, we should join with other women to fight the things that put us down. It's not easy, but we can only win the fight by sticking together.

You might be able to find books in the library about Sexism, or Women's Liberation. Ask the librarian to help you, or ask a woman teacher you think might help, or just start talking about it with some of the other girls in your class.

What aren't you allowed to do just because you're a girl? Probably lots of things. What about the things mentioned above?

A group of you may decide that you want to play football. You could start by telling the principal or some of the teachers that you think it's unfair.

You might not get things changed quickly but you will find out who's on your side, and who isn't. Finding them feels really great. There are lots of people on your side, it's just a matter of finding them. Good Luck.

Discovering my lesbianism

by Mary Ann Deutschmann

B.IRELAND

I don't want to create a separation between myself and other women because I identify myself as a lesbian. I feel that we have many of the same everyday battles, and share a lot of the same kinds of problems with our sexuality. Being in the shit work world is difficult for me, as it is for all women. At my last job as a maid in a hospital, I had an added pressure because I feared that I would lose my job if it was known that I was a lesbian. But the main problems were the low-paid 40 hour a week drudgery and the degradation by men that I shared with all the other maids.

I was confronted with situations every day there that put me in my place. Sometimes I failed to stand up for myself and other times I'd take care of myself well. I experienced a lot of insults, condescension, teasing and general disrespect which made me see what men really think of women. These men for the most part were very friendly and 'nice,' which made them harder to deal with. My boss, for instance, was very friendly, but he often made me feel like shit. He called the housekeepers "my girls" and teased me about everything he could discover about my life. It hooked me into laughing back at the teasing, which wasn't at all what I felt like doing.

Only twice did I ever verbally express anger; one day when he called me 'cutie,' and another time when he told me that "riding your bicycle should trim your waistline." But I did begin to learn to keep that perpetual smile off my face, which used to automatically appear whether I felt like smiling or not. This really unnerved some men. They couldn't get my smile of approval for the 'groovy' sexist things they said — so their ego was deflated just a bit.

Being a lesbian has to do with my sexuality, although I am not, as one man harshly told me, "making a limited decision for your life based on sex!" Sex is a really hard thing for me. I built up many blocks about sex while growing up because of a lack of information, not understanding my body or men's bodies, the suppression of my sexual attraction to women, guilt from my religious beliefs, and an environment in which people do not freely touch each other. Although this set of experiences is normal for many children growing up in our society, they were forced into the extreme for me. I am the daughter of a minister, and when I was in grade school the other kids completely excluded me from any talk of sex because of it. This, and everything else about being a 'preacher's kid' blew my worries about sex out of proportion.

Before I ever had sex with a woman, I had bad sexual experiences with men. One time this happened with Adam, a man who I really loved. We had a friendship in which we tried to be as honest and supportive of each other as we knew how to be. Our relationship had never been sexual, but I was starved for more physical closeness with him. So one night, after drinking a lot of wine, I became very aggressive with him and we ended up in bed together. At first I felt very giving and happy to be with him. But soon I became very threatened. I felt pressure and numbness. This was Sex and I felt that now a lot was demanded of me. I had never shared with anyone the consuming fears and worries I'd been having for years about sex. How could I suddenly make myself vulnerable and open? Without any explanation I abruptly left him. I didn't understand my feelings and I had no idea how to be honest about them. The experience was destructive to both of us and our relationship deteriorated.

At least Adam had been as sensitive as he knew how to be, and had not pressured me about sex. But he was an exception. All around me I saw men who were completely insensitive to women's feelings. I saw my best friend being constantly pressured to have sex, even when the men knew she was confused. I spent hours being an understanding listener to men although they didn't try very hard to get into my feelings. Yet they expected me to be sexually free with them. That kind of pressure and insensitivity was just the opposite of what I needed.

Through all of this, my relationships with my women friends were much more supportive and important to me. But they caused me a lot of pain and guilt because I knew that I was attracted to them. I tried very hard to lie to myself about this, but it was impossible to block.

My feelings about myself and my sexuality changed a lot when I began to explore them with other women in a women's group. In sharing my experiences and hearing other women talk about theirs, I grew to value the special understanding that women have among themselves. I stopped hating myself so much when I understood my conditioning. I saw that we could help each other change. I accepted for myself that loving women was an important and vital part of me. It was much more real than my desires to be like everyone else and to have a boyfriend.

Who are our friends?

Only a gay person knows what it's like to be gay. But many people understand what it's like to be treated unfairly. These are the people who are likely to be on our side.

A lot of women, for instance, even if they're not gay, know what gay people are up against. Just as the church and the law try to run gay people's lives, they also try to make all women have children whether they want them or not. A lot of the straight men who put down women are the same ones who make life hard for all gay people. The people who say it's not natural for people of the same sex to love each other will often say it's not natural if women don't want to get married and have children.

The lies spread about women are like the lies spread about all gay people. Women are supposed to be weaker than men, and they're all meant to enjoy doing housework. A lot of women are starting to say that these *are* lies and are putting the record right. Some of the women are lesbians, some aren't. All of these women are likely to understand what we're saying and stick up for us. We should stick up for them too.

Others who get a bad time for no good reason are blacks, Chicanos, immigrants, poor people and the unemployed. If you're one of these people you'll know the feeling. You get called names like nigger, spic, welfare parasite... which are meant to give the idea that what you are is no good. Isn't that just what names like dyke and faggot are supposed to do too!

One thing to remember though. Just because people are treated unfairly does not always mean that they are our friends. Often you'll find that mistreated people believe the lies about all other groups *except* their own. There are white gay people who put down blacks, just as there are blacks who put down gays.

It's not hard to understand why this happens. If people are made to feel worthless they often look for someone to take it out on. It's hard to fight back against the things that make people feel worthless, and sometimes it's hard to pick what they are (like the law, the church, the newspaper owners, the politicians, big businessmen). So these people look around for someone weaker than themselves to kick. If there's no dog around, it might be gay people they kick. That doesn't mean it's right. It's just something we have to watch out for.

There are also people who go on believing the lies even about their own group. If they're in power, these are really dangerous people. For instance, there are gay politicians who vote against homosexual law reform. Or gay shrinks who tell other gays they're sick just for being gay. These people are more interested in running the place than they are in helping

other gays. They certainly are not *our* friends.

Our only hope of getting a fair deal is when we join with all the other groups who are fighting for their rights. On our own we are a small group, but when many groups get together — racial minorities, unemployed people, gays, migrant workers — then we are the majority. There are more of us than of them. When we're all together we can fight back and win!

HUMAN RIGHTS

DYKES UNITE

B.IRELAND

Getting by

The first thing we all have to do is find a way of getting by. A way to keep alive — and kicking!

At school most of us are dead scared if we think we're gay. Some of us decide to act quiet. We try not to give anything away about ourselves. Some of us become bookworms. We bury ourselves in schoolwork so we'll forget what we're feeling inside. Some of us push ourselves in other ways. Some get stuck into sport. Some become monitors. Some help teachers with this and that. Some of us put all our energy into acting more straight than the straights, so no one will guess.

If we act in any of these ways we are often just trying to push our gay feelings to one side. That may work, but only for a while. Doing these things certainly won't help us if we're feeling uptight.

If you are finding it hard at the moment, you may sometimes wish you were straight. You may have heard of so-called "cures" for homosexuality. Well, there's no such thing. *Not one* of these "cures" has *ever* been shown to work! And what's more, they are extremely cruel. They're not much better than torture. Don't let anyone kid you about them. You just can't make a gay person straight.

We have to learn to face up to our gay feelings. And not to feel worried about them. They won't go away if we ignore them. But why should we want them to?

There are lots of books you can read written by gay people about being gay. They'll give you useful information, and make you feel better about being gay yourself. You'll find some of these books listed at the back of this one. Records are listed there too.

You can also find out what the gay groups in your city (or nearest city) are doing.

Finding these groups may be hard; some advice about how to do it is in the back of this book. Write to them, or phone them, even if you feel you're not ready yet to mix with other gay people. Even a little contact can be reassuring.

It's great if we're lucky enough to have some friends around us who will help us and back us up. They give help in ways that parents and families often can't. Friends are important for us all our lives.

But, of course, friends can only really help us if they know we're gay. A lot of people find the best way of getting by is to come right out and tell people. That's not easy. We know. But the next chapter will give you some clues on how to go about it, and why it's helpful. And important.

Telling other people

So you feel the world is against you? Are you afraid of what will happen if other people find out you're gay? You think other people at school will start making jokes about you? They'll call you a dyke or a pervert or fairy or faggot. They might even beat you up. You'll lose your friends. And what if your parents find out?

Well, stop being afraid. We know that as gay people we're just as good as the rest of them!

Just remember that. And then you'll start getting ready to *say* so. We're not going to say you won't have some real hassles, but you're going to feel much better if you learn to be proud and fight back.

For a start, *not* everyone is against gay people. In fact, most people are only repeating the lies and put-downs they have heard all around them, without ever having thought about what they are saying. Like the people at school who put down "wops" — and have a best friend with an Italian or Greek name!

It *is* easier for you when you don't feel you've got to hide who you really are all the time. Doing that only makes you hate yourself as a phoney. Nearly every gay person has been through this. Especially at school. You're not alone.

Whenever one of us stand up and says we're glad and proud to be gay — even to one other person — it makes it easier for the rest of us. And it gives us an example worth living up to. So when we show we're not afraid, we're helping other gays too. And it's one way of finding out who the other gay people are.

The people you're going to want to tell are probably those you feel closest to. The first time you'll probably be feeling dead scared. But when you feel ready, and you think the time is right, do it. It really is like lifting a lead weight off your back. You'll feel really proud of yourself. And for a while you'll probably find you get a real kick out of telling people. Who knows... you'll want to paint it on walls!

There's no one way. Some of us do it gradually. We start giving our hints — sounding out people's attitudes, asking them if they've got any gay friends, perhaps loaning them a good book that we've just read. Often then they will guess, and think about it, before we get to tell them.

Another way of telling people is when we're asked questions like "Do you think you'll ever be getting married?" If it's someone you can trust, you can say in a matter of fact way, "No, I won't be getting married." If they ask, "Why?" and you feel *now* is the moment, then say that it's because you're gay.

Deciding who to tell and when is something only you can know about. Of course, it's going to be more difficult telling some people than others. Just use your common sense.

Are you worried about your straight friends? You don't want them to freak out and just walk out on you. But you'd like to be able to talk to them about the things you really feel. So when you tell them, make them think about it. How they take it is really *their* worry. They may need a bit of time to get used to the idea, but if they're any friends at all, they'll stick with you, and they will think about it. If they stop being friends because you're gay, it'll annoy you — but at least you'll know that *they're* wrong. Eventually they're going to have to get their heads sorted out. You're not the only gay person they're going to meet.

Sometimes, you're right. It would be safer to shut up about it. If you think someone's going to bash you for saying you're gay, why shouldn't you be careful? But why shouldn't you be angry, too? There's no reason why we should have to run away or hide because we're gay. So it's a good idea to start getting ready to stick up for yourself, ready to fight back if you ever have to. You'll take people by surprise because they won't be expecting you to fight back.

I came out in class

by Ron Schettino

All through high school, I disliked getting up for school and waiting for the bus. I liked the bus ride in, though.

A lot of people made gay jokes about each other. Nobody thought that anybody was actually gay, but the jokes were popular. For example: "Hey, Schettino! Who's queerer, you or your husband?" I laughed along with the rest of them, but nobody suspected that I really was gay.

The kids on the bus made a lot of gay jokes at everybody on the bus.

The bus pulled into the school parking lot; we were dropped off at the smoking area. Almost everybody had a cigarette in their hand. I squeezed my way through the crowd, and worked my way into the cafeteria to wait for homeroom. Every day, for four years, it was the same — until I decided to change it.

All my life I had known I was gay and had kept it to myself.

Two months before graduation I came out to my family. Their reactions were surprising, just the opposite of how I thought they'd react: they took the news quite well. I began dating a guy, Howard, who is now my lover. I saw how well my family took the news and decided to tell my close friends at school.

My father warned me that I shouldn't come out at school to anybody. He told me that news of it would spread like wildfire and I'd get into trouble. I just had to see for myself.

A month before graduation I found myself sitting in class, not being able to work. I had Howard, my boyfriend, on my mind all day and I didn't want to keep my homosexuality to myself any longer.

There were three people sitting around me, two of whom were good friends, Emily and Mark. The third, Wendy, was a junior who I didn't know very well.

"Emily," I began, "I have

something I think I want to tell you." (I chose to start with Emily because I knew that she had a gay friend in junior high school.)

"What is it?" asked Emily.

Wendy and Mark were listening closely.

"I'm not sure how to tell you this." (And I wasn't.) "You've noticed I've been happier the past two weeks. I've changed."

"Yeah," she said, "I noticed a change."

"Well, I don't know how to say this..."

"Try!" said Wendy.

"O.K.... I met this great person and fell in love last weekend."

"Oh?!" said Emily. "Do I know her?"

"It's not a her," I said. Everyone's eyes in the room went up.

"You're bisexual?" asked Emily.

"No, guess again."

Just then another student, who must have been listening, put his arms on my desk, looked right into my eyes and asked, quite loudly, "You're gay?!" The class fell silent.

All I could do was nod my head 'yes.'

He stood up quickly and exclaimed, "What?!"

"Don't tell him!" exclaimed Wendy. The teacher looked over. "He'll tell the world." I didn't really seem to care.

Mark looked over to me and asked quietly, "Are you really gay?"

"Yes," I said.

"I always wanted to know one, and find out more about you people," he said.

"You people?!" I said. "I'm me people, I'm the same person I was the last four years."

"I'm really happy for you," said Emily. "Not that you're gay, that doesn't matter. I'm happy that you fell in love."

Emily and Wendy began asking questions about Howard, like where is he from, where did I meet him, where does he work. I was ready to answer all of their questions.

Mark asked me questions about my sex life. The only answer I had for him was that I enjoyed sexual relationships with men.

The people in the class weren't bothered about the news too much. The news did spread, but I didn't get too many hassles from the other students. The people who were prejudiced didn't bother me, they just didn't talk to me.

Some people I didn't want to find out would hear it from someone else. They would come up to me and ask me if it was true.

"What do you think?" I asked them.

None of them believed it, so for them, I left it like that. But with any real friends, I was much happier knowing I didn't have to keep secrets from them any longer.

A lesbian in class!

by Beth Harrison

This spring I came out in high school. It was one of the hardest things I've done in my life, and it caused a lot of problems, but in the long run I've gained more than I lost.

The way it happened is that my sociology teacher, who is very liberal, was having a special unit on minorities — and one of them was homosexuals. One day he had in a lesbian and two gay men to talk to the class. Everyone had a lot of questions: "Do you want to adopt children?" "Are you attracted to every woman you meet?" (This was asked by a girl in the class to the lesbian, who said "No, are you?") "How can you say you're discriminated against when you can look and act like everybody else if you want to?" "When did you first know you were gay?"

Most kids were very curious, and they didn't seem to really dislike the speakers; they just didn't know what to make of them.

At one point, one of the men said "There's 22 students in this room. It's pretty likely that two of you are gay." Everybody looked around at everybody else. I don't think anybody really believed that any of *us* were gay. By then I was feeling good about my lesbianism, though, and I had seen that no one else in the class was really hostile toward the gay speakers. I had been thinking for a long time about coming out to people in school and I decided, well, it's now or never! So I raised my hand. "That's right," I said. "I'm one of them." (I just couldn't quite get myself to say "I'm a lesbian.")

Everybody was silent. Even the gay speakers didn't know what to say for a minute. Some people were obviously bothered, and I clearly remember one girl, who I didn't really know, who scooted her chair back away from me and looked distinctly disgusted. But in a few minutes people were asking me questions. The next day, everybody in school knew.

What's happened now? Well, the lesbian speaker (her name is Madge) was very helpful. She talked to me after school for a long time, and we talked about the problems I was going to face, and how good it felt to be honest with everybody for once, and about dozens of other things. Without her, my life would have been much harder.

In school, most of my friends didn't change how they acted with me. Some of them would talk to me about it, though, and some wouldn't. One girl that I knew (thought I knew) very well wouldn't have anything to do with me, and some of the boys thought it was pretty cool to put me down, as if they couldn't have anything to do with a girl who didn't want to go out with them. I found "DYKE" scrawled on my locker once. I just left it there and tried to pretend I didn't care, though I did sometimes.

So there were good and bad results. But I know I've been honest with myself and with everybody else, and my true friends are still my friends. I thought a few other lesbians might turn up in school. So far they haven't, but I know I've made it easier for any that want to come out later. And I've met Madge, who is now my very best friend. Coming out was a monumental event for me, but it was worth it all.

Telling your parents

Telling parents might be the hardest bit, and it's going to depend a lot on what kind of people they are. *You* will know this best. Yes, there are some parents who will crack up, and just refuse to accept you for what you are. There are some parents who will just pretend that they haven't heard what you said, and that nothing has happened. There are some parents who will say they don't mind, but only so long as your aunt or your granny or the neighbors never find out!

But there are some parents who *really* don't mind. They'll accept you for who you are. They may even help you. There is a group called Parents of Gays with chapters in many cities, that is working along with us to make things better.

Whenever you tell your parents, or anyone, in fact, it's a good idea to have lots of information about gay people ready to tell them. You'll find some things to tell them from this book, and more in the books listed at the back of this one.

But if you know you have the kind of parents who would say, "My daughter's going to get married," or "No son of mine's going to be a goddamned fairy," maybe it's better to wait till you leave school and aren't dependent on them. But if you do tell them, or they find out, and they act like this, try to stay cool and talk about it with them. If that doesn't work, you could go for help to good friends or other relatives who understand, or to one of the gay groups listed at the back of this book. But *never* let your parents — or anyone else — make you ashamed of who you are!

It pays to stop and think about why our parents are acting in the way they are. Often they're afraid for themselves. They're afraid other people will think they've failed as parents because their kid is different. They may want us to do just what they did, and they're refusing to think that any other kind of life is good for us. Like other people they may try to scare us into thinking that if we don't get married, we'll be lonely.

Well, for a start, everyone's lonely sometimes. Even our parents. That's just a fact.

But what's so special about the way our parents live anyway? Today more and more people are finding out that it's better for them not to live in a marriage or an old-style family. Some people like to live on their own.

Others live in houses with groups of friends and share the food and the housework. Living in one of these ways can give us the chance to deal with people how and when we want to, instead of being tied to someone whether we like it or not, just because we thought that was how everybody had to live.

If you're a young woman, you'll know that it's you and your mother who get to do all the shit-jobs for all the men who are around. You'll be glad you don't have to do things like that for some man.

If you're a young gay man, you can be helping work out new ways of being friends with women, ways that don't put them down all the time like the straight guys you know are often doing.

A letter to parents

Dear Mom & Dad,
I read in the paper the other day that a mother marched in a New York Gay Liberation parade carrying a sign that said, "I am proud of my gay son." Since telling you that I am gay, I've been wondering if you are still proud of me. And if you are, I wonder *why* you are

HELP SUPPORT
WITH PRIDE
OUR GAY
CHILDREN

B. IRELAND

proud. A lot of your friends and neighbors seem to be proud of their children just because they have been to college, because they have a new brick veneer house, because the girls have married rich men, because they have holidays in the Bahamas. That seems rather silly to me. Maybe it's because you brought me up to put people first and possessions second. If you are proud of me I hope it's because of who I am and not what I own.

Or are you ashamed of me just because I am homosexual? Being heterosexual is not an achievement and neither is being homosexual. It just happens. But being homosexual in a hostile society does take a bit of courage. It can be quite dangerous. Maybe for that reason you wish I was heterosexual, just as you would rather I didn't become a racing car driver, because that's pretty dangerous too. But you see, that's why I'm in Gay Liberation, because I want to make it happier and safer to be homosexual.

One of the things that I have learnt from the gay liberation movement is that homo-

sexuality is not a defect or a disease. There is nothing wrong with being homosexual. I think that you accept this easily enough where other people's children are concerned, but when it comes to me you ask, "Where did we go wrong? Who is to blame?" The simple and happy answer is that no one went wrong and there is no one to blame. If you don't look at it as a problem, it ceases to be a problem.

And despite all the social pressures, I am happy. I think you can see that. I am happy because I accept myself and I live the way I want to.

There is a generation gap, just because the world is changing so fast. And that means that we both have to be very patient and listen to each other's point of view. Your opinion means a lot to me. Recently some people from Gay Liberation were talking at a high school about homosexuals and their parents, and one of the other guest speakers said that children didn't care what their parents thought these days. The high school pupils all disagreed with her. They said they might pretend not to, but they cared very much what their parents thought of them.

I am very glad that I have told you that I am homosexual. It is a great weight off my mind and it is much easier for me to talk to you now that I have nothing to hide. It wasn't easy for me to tell you. I was pretty scared because I know of cases where parents had threatened their children, turned them out of the house, or dragged them off to see psychiatrists. They did not stop to consider how painful and degrading the psychiatric treatment was, that it can have dreadful side effects and that it hardly ever alters homosexual behavior. No wonder Gay Liberation talks about oppression, when some of us are persecuted in our own homes and rejected by our families. I really can't say how glad I am that you didn't react that way.

When you meet my homosexual friends you will notice that they are nothing like the homosexuals described in the sensational Sunday papers or made fun of in the comedies on television. Did you think they would be? There are lies told about us all the time, and often we dare not answer back because if we do we will lose our jobs or our friends.

Like many other people, we in Gay Liberation are starting to question the old ideas about marriage and the family. Some of us may have children (homosexuals do have children, you know), but we are not likely to marry and we think that the family has many faults. But when I criticize the family I am not criticizing you personally. I am saying that I think children should not always be expected to be like their parents (i.e. get married and raise a family). Still I know that you have done your best for me. You are two people I know very well and love very much.

Your child,
Richard

Changing things

During the past ten years, a great many straight people have come to realize that homosexuals do face discrimination. Some cities and states have outlawed discrimination against gays in housing or employment. Does this mean that it is any easier to be gay now than it was 10 years ago?

Yes and no. Many more people agree now that gays should not be treated as criminals. But many of those same people think that homosexuality is wrong, or at least not as good as hetero-sexuality.

The attitude of the Catholic Church is a good example. Many Catholic groups have agreed that homosexuality should not be a crime. But the Catholic Church still says that homosexuality is a *sin* and a *disorder*.

Lesbians know all about this. Sex between women has never been a crime in some areas. But lesbians share many of the problems that gay men have in dealing with family, jobs, insults on the street, etc.

So does this mean nothing has changed?

Not quite. Ten years ago there were hardly any openly gay people around. Now there are quite a few. Gays are coming out on T.V., telling their friends — many of us are sick and tired of hiding. The effect is that a lot more people are able to see what real live lesbians and gay men are like. People who thought they had never met a gay person find that that's not true. When a best friend turns out to be gay, it's not so easy to believe the lies and wild stories flying round about gay people.

How will things get better?

Every time you tell someone you're gay, it makes it that much easier for us all. *What we need to work at is making it easier for all gays to be open.*

Changes in the law do help —

but obviously they are not enough.

We need laws that make it a crime for employers or landlords to discriminate against gay people. Laws like this have been passed in Quebec and in many American cities.

We need more unions to take a stand in support of their gay members. Some teachers' unions have done this already.

We need more radio and TV stations to have special programs for their gay listeners. We also need programs that are useful in reaching the hetero-sexuals who are on our side.

We need sex education in schools that talks about gay sexuality without putting it down, and where gays can have a fair say.

All these are ways that will make it easier for gay people to come out. The question is: *How can we help make these things happen?*

The first thing to do is to find our friends — the people who hate injustice and who will do what they can to stop it.

Working with others is a lot more effective — strength in numbers! It's usually more fun too.

At school we can:
• Find out who the OK people are, other kids, teachers, etc.
• Read up on homosexuality — so that you can back up what you say whenever you need to.
• See what can be done about getting good books into the library or getting good sex education courses going.
• Find out how to go about getting gay speakers in to talk about being gay with students or with teachers.
• If someone is getting picked on for being gay, see what you and your friends can do about it.
• If you have a school newspaper write something for it about being gay. That's worth doing even if you don't sign it. At least they'll know there are gay people around!

Outside school we can:
• Make contact with a gay group (see list at the end of book). This is a way of meeting others with ideas about things that can be done. For instance

some groups produce posters and buttons that say things like, "How dare you presume I'm heterosexual," or "Homosexuality — why settle for less." They also produce leaflets, run conferences and dances, write letters to the papers, talk on TV, etc. They even write booklets for use in schools! These are the people to contact for speakers to come out to schools.

• Once you leave school, if you get a job you'll probably join a union. You might get involved in other groups like community groups, sports groups, or political groups. Find out who the gay people are in these groups, get together and start working to get the group to support its gay members.

So you can see there's no end to what you can do. First, find your friends, then get together and get started!

Doing it — gay men

There are lots of different ways for gay men to have sex and to really enjoy it. You will soon find out what *you* like and how you like to do it.

The first thing you should do is to find out all about your own body. Get to know it and get to like it. Use a mirror for all those hard places to see.

You have probably jerked off (masturbated). This is really just making love with yourself and it's a great feeling, isn't it? Masturbation is also a great way of finding out how good sex can be. Don't worry about doing it. It's absolutely harmless. Almost *everybody* masturbates, gay and straight, teenagers, adults, males and females. People get uptight about it because they don't like the idea of young people enjoying sex.

The sex education books in your school are all written by heterosexuals, and they will tell you that the only way for a man to enjoy sex is when he is having intercourse (fucking) with a woman. That is, when his penis (cock) is in her vagina. This just isn't true. Not even for straight people!

Gay men can make love in many different ways. Here are a few examples:
• kissing, cuddling, stroking, and holding somebody close.
• jerking each other off, either together or in turns.
• sucking each other's penises, either doing it at the same time or taking it in turns. Because mouths are soft and warm, having your penis sucked feels really good. If you are doing the sucking, hold the other person's penis with one hand, and put it gently into your mouth. It feels nice and smooth. Run your tongue up and down it towards the tip, and try and watch out your teeth don't get in the way too much... they're hard. Don't worry about swallowing the semen. It just tastes salty. And it's perfectly harmless.

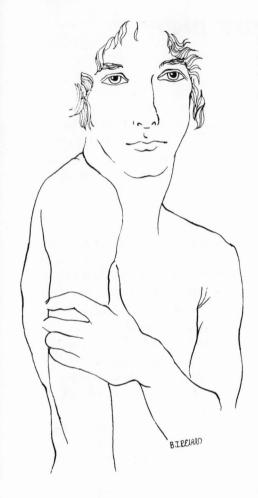

B.IRELAND

By the way, don't get hung up about the size or shape of your penis, whether you think it's too big or too small. The size of your penis doesn't prove how much of a "man" you are in any way at all. The size of your penis has also got nothing to do with how much you enjoy sex or how much enjoyment you give to another person.

And try not to worry about when — or even if — you have an orgasm (come)! After all, sex is still enjoyable even if you don't actually have an orgasm. These things only seem a problem if you are feeling uptight about the situation you're in. You both have to feel relaxed to enjoy sex completely.

Because such a big deal is made by heterosexuals about men having intercourse with women, a lot of people think that for gay men having anal intercourse (ass fucking) with each other is the only way to enjoy sex. This isn't true. Anal intercourse is just one way of having sex. There's nothing special about it. You may find you like this kind of sex with other men best of all, or you may not like it especially. It's up to you. Just experiment and do what you like, and make sure you're not forced into doing anything.

Perhaps there are some men who only enjoy taking the so-called "active" part in intercourse (doing the fucking), and some men who only enjoy the "passive" part (being fucked). But *most* like it *both ways*. It's good taking it in turns to play the "active" part with each other. But there are no rules. It all depends on what you both want and what you learn from each other.

If you are taking the "passive" part, and you feel worried that your partner is trying to put you down or play power-games with you by having intercourse, make sure you tell him first, so you can both talk about it. And make sure if you are taking the "active" part, you yourself are not playing power-games. You must always remember that you are making love to another person like yourself, and not just another penis or anus. Sex is something for you *both* to enjoy.

You have probably been told as you have grown up that your anus is a dirty place and shouldn't be touched. This is stupid. People should be happy with *all* parts of their bodies.

It is true that you get rid of waste out of your anus, but that's not the only thing that it's good for. You pass urine (piss) out of your penis too, but you can do more things with your penis than that. Your anus is only dirty when it hasn't been cleaned — just like any other part of your body.

Your anus is not only an organ to remove waste. It can be sexually exciting, just like your penis, because it has a lot of sensitive nerve-endings around the outside and also inside it, just like the nerves at the top of your penis. When these nerve-endings are being touched or stroked it can really turn you on.

You don't have to have intercourse to enjoy the feelings of your anus. You can use fingers, either your own or someone else's. Try using your fingers to begin with and you will soon see what we mean. Be a bit careful the first time though, and never put anything else up your anus, as this can be dangerous. Also it is a good idea to use something slippery when having sex this

way, such as baby oil or Vaseline. You can use spit when there is nothing else around.

If you find anal intercourse a little hard, it may be because it is not your thing. Or it might be that you need to practice a bit for the pleasure to come through, just like anything else that's new. Don't get hung up about it. Like we said, it's just one way of enjoying sex among lots of others.

There are gay sex books around now that really go into details. But really all you both need to do is to relax, take things gently at first, and enjoy the excitement of being close to the person you are having sex with.

Learning how to give and receive love through warm and enjoyable sex is one of the best ways of showing the world how much we like ourselves and each other.

It also shows the straight world that they are not going to force us to live according to their narrow-minded ideas. There are lots of stories about men and sex. Men are supposed to take a pride in how many different people they have had sex with, for instance. Well, that's *not* important. Men are even supposed to be proud of making someone have sex with them who doesn't really want to. That's an unforgivable thing to do. It's just the kind of stupid idea we can do without! As gay men we should be showing the world we can be loving to each other, and that all those stories about what "real" men are meant to be like are just a load of bullshit.

Doing it — lesbians

B. IRELAND

Well, the first thing we want to say about lesbian loving is that there aren't any rules and we don't want any.

There are lots of ways you can make love to a woman and we will mention just a few of them, but the first place to start is with you. The first woman you should start loving is yourself. That might sound strange, but you have to feel happy about yourself and about your own body before you can feel good with someone else.

One of the ways you can get to know your own body is by masturbating. Masturbation is simply you making love to yourself because it feels good. By itself it's going to make you feel good and it will probably give you ideas about what other women might like. Some of us like being kissed all over, some of us don't. Some of us like having our breasts touched, kissed, licked; some of us don't. Like we've said, there aren't any rules.

Probably all the sex-education books at your school were written by *heterosexuals* (people who have sexual relations with their opposite sex) and they probably show diagrams like the one shown here, but talk mainly about your *vagina* as being the most important place.

There are a lot of heterosexual people who think that the only real sex is when the man's penis is inside the vagina of the woman. But this isn't true, even for heterosexuals. We know that the clitoris is one of the most sexually sensitive and responsive parts of our bodies.

Being a lesbian means exploring. Explore your own body, touch it, look at it, use a mirror to explore the parts you can't see easily. Get to know yourself and explore the woman you're with, sexually, emotionally, totally.

Ḃut you still want us to tell you how to do it, right?

Well, here are a few ideas, but they aren't all there is.

First, fingers. Using your fingers, try caressing the *labia*, running them around the whole area, inside the vagina, out again and up to the clitoris until sexual excitation or orgasm happens. You can do this to each other at the same time or take it in turns.

You can use your tongue. You could trace the edges of her labia, kiss and push at her clitoris with your tongue, and you can both do this at the same time, too.

Another way of making love is to just lie together, one on top of the other and use the friction of one body on another.

Well, that's just three ideas which seem to be fairly common ones. However, use your imagination, and just keep doing what feels good.

Something to remember about orgasms — yes they're good and make you feel great but sometimes you can feel just as good without an orgasm. You don't have to have an orgasm to "prove" that you're feeling great about the other person and you don't have to feel guilty if she doesn't have an orgasm.

Now you're not going to be

the world's greatest lover at your first attempt. So what? Practice in this case doesn't make perfect but it does help. You and the woman you're with will work out what feels good for each of you. That means a lot of honest talking between the two of you about what you like and what you don't, in all parts of your feelings for each other, not just the sexual ones.

So it all comes back to exploring.

All women, whether we are lesbians or not, need to explore ourselves. We need to use our talents. We should ask ourselves a few questions.

Is life for a woman, for me, just going to be me married, a housewife, or a secretary for men as most people expect me to be? As a lesbian you might not get married (although there are some married women and mothers who are lesbians), but you will have to make some hard decisions. You'll have to fight a lot because you will be doing something that men don't like and there are many things that are hard for women in the world the way it is now, because men don't like us doing them. As lesbians and as women we have to fight this. We have fought to choose a different way of living. We feel great about it, and we think you will too.

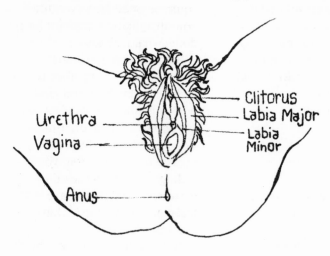

Meeting other gays

Dear friends,

I'm seventeen, and for almost a year now I've known I am a lesbian. Actually I've known for a lot longer than that, but I never would have actually used the words "lesbian" or "homosexual" to describe myself until recently.

My problem is simple. I don't know a single other lesbian in the world. I've never even slept with another girl although I know I would like to sometime.

I told one of my teachers about myself once. I thought she would be helpful, and she was very understanding, but she has a boyfriend and all that. I have some good friends at school, boys and girls both, and we have good times together, but sometimes I feel so alone! Like nobody understands or even knows the real me. What can I do?

Kathy

Dear Kathy,

It can be very difficult for young gay people to meet others, especially if your parents are strict about letting you out of the house, or if you live in a small town and have trouble getting to any larger cities.

There are several things that may help, though. Since the late 1960s, women involved in the women's liberation and gay movements have been building communication and support networks. In most cities or towns you can find a women's community center or women's health clinic, or something similar. Get in touch with them. They'll be able to tell you about activities they're organizing, and will probably know about places where lesbians hang out.

Often, they'll be organizing support groups, consciousness-raising groups, or workshops. You can probably find other lesbians who would like to start a lesbian support group.

As you meet other lesbians, you'll find that they are creating new forms of relationships. Don't feel like you have to approach a relationship in the same way that heterosexual people do. Follow your feelings and your beliefs about how you really want to be with someone. Most gay people find that they need both a lover (or lovers) and close gay friends with whom they have non-sexual relationships.

Larger cities usually have a gay organization that acts as a clearinghouse, keeping track of the activities and groups that are available for people like you. They may be listed in the phone book under Gay Hotline or Gay Community Center or something similar. If there's nothing in the city where you live, check the nearest larger city; even if it's too far away for you to travel to regularly, someone there may be able to help you get in touch with individuals or groups closer to you. You'll find that most gays, once you describe your situation, will be eager to help you meet others. After all, they've been through much the same situation!

The more you can talk to people about your gayness, the fewer problems you're likely to have because of it. When people finally stop thinking about homosexuality as some exotic disease, they'll be less likely to block out their own gay feelings. You may find that coming out in school eventually helps you meet some gay classmates!

Dear Friends,
I had my first gay experience a year ago. I am pretty happy about being gay. Even though I'm underage I have no trouble getting into bars, and I've met some great guys that way. But all of them are five or ten years older than me. I sure would like to know some boys my age who are gay.
John

Dear John,
Finding other young gays can be especially hard. The suggestions above will help, though some of them apply only to women.

In a few cities there are gay youth groups where it's easy to meet other young gays in a relaxed setting. If you live in a city that doesn't have such a group, but that has an adult gay liberation organization, approach them and see if someone there would help you start a gay youth group.

Unfortunately, in most cases there will be no such group around. You'll have to manage with what already exists. Ask around until you know about all the different bars, organizations, etc., where gay people meet in your city. Some of them may have more young people than others. Try different places until you find one that's got a crowd and atmosphere you like.

As long as our society makes it so hard for young people to recognize and be open about their sexuality, though, the fact is there just won't be too many young gay people out there for you to meet. And that brings up a final suggestion for you to think about: coming out to friends and classmates at school. It's difficult, and it may not be the sensible thing to do in your situation, but it's worth considering.

Scattered through this book you'll find lots of thoughts about that. The thing to remember is that when you tell people you're gay, it's an important experience for you — and also for them.

Your friends, who have known and liked you as a person, will realize that homosexuality isn't some distant thing that only affects strangers. They'll realize that if you can be gay, so can lots of other people — they may even start to think more about their own sexuality, and realize that they have more choices than they had known.

Once people have gotten over the initial surprise or shock, they'll have plenty of questions for you — some hostile, others friendly and wanting to understand more. Learn to ignore the hostile ones, but try to be patient and helpful for the others, and encourage them to ask about what they don't understand. People are afraid when something seems very foreign and strange to them.

Gays and health

There are diseases that can be spread through sexual contact with other people. These are called venereal diseases (V.D.)

V.D. can affect all people — straight or gay. There is nothing about gay sex itself that makes us more or less likely than heterosexuals to get V.D. However, V.D. is very rare among lesbians.

There are many types of venereal disease, but two of the most common — and most dangerous — are gonorrhea and syphilis.

Gonorrhea and syphilis germs live only in warm moist places like the vagina, penis or anus. They can be spread whenever an affected penis, mouth, anus or vagina comes in contact with the penis, mouth, anus or vagina of another person.

Gonorrhea and syphilis are *not* spread by towels, toilet seats, etc. The germs that cause these diseases cannot live outside the body for more than a few seconds.

Both gonorrhea and syphilis are easily cured, but if not treated they can cause serious harm to the body (especially syphilis). The first signs of these diseases sometimes go away even if not treated. This does *not* mean the disease is cured. It is therefore very important to recognize the signs of either one as soon as they appear.

As soon as you know you have gonorrhea or syphilis, make sure you tell all the people you might have given it to, so they can get treatment. Avoid having sex again until the doctor tells you you're cured. You should also avoid alcohol, which can affect the medicine used for treating V.D.

It's possible to have one of these diseases without knowing it. You might only find out when you give it to someone else. The only sure way to protect yourself and others is to have regular check-ups for V.D. every three to six months.

If you are in a steady sexual relationship with one person, and that person doesn't have sex with anyone else, then the risk of catching V.D. is very small. Otherwise there is a real risk, and a routine check-up is necessary.

When you go for a V.D. check, always tell the doctor that you're gay when that is relevant. Many doctors do not check a man's throat or anus for V.D. unless asked to do so.

You don't become immune to syphilis or gonorrhea just because you've had them once. You can get either disease again, simply by sexual contact with someone who's infected.

There are several other venereal diseases that you should know about.

Non Specific Urethritis (known as NSU) is a common condition that affects men. Its cause is not known.

NSU is similar to gonorrhea, especially in its early stages. The signs are a discharge (usually clear) from the penis, plus mild pain when urinating.

It is possible to have NSU and gonorrhea at the same time, and the usual treatment for gonorrhea (penicillin) does *not* cure NSU.

Sometimes the treatment for NSU is to avoid sex until the symptoms are gone, and for about a month after that. More often doctors will prescribe antibiotics.

Avoid alcohol if you have NSU. It seems that alcohol prolongs the infection.

NSU is contagious, so all partners should be contacted. Although NSU is less serious than gonorrhea, it must never be ignored. For one thing, untreated NSU can spread and do damage to other parts of the body. For another, it may not be NSU — it may be gonorrhea.

Cystitus is a urinary tract infection that mainly affects women, although lesbians are less likely to get it than are heterosexual women. Since the urinary opening is just under the clitoris, it can easily be

How to tell you have it

Gonorrhea:
Symptoms show up 2-28 days after sexual contact. There are *no* symptoms for 50-80% of infected women, and for 5-10% of infected men.
•In the penis:
Discharge or drip from the penis. Stinging feeling when urinating.
•In the vagina:
May be a greenish discharge. Burning feeling around lips of vagina.
Often no symptoms.
•In the anus:
Often no symptoms except for discomfort, soreness or pain. Sometimes an anal discharge shows up on underwear. Perhaps itching, pus or blood in feces (shit), diarrhea.

Syphilis:
Symptoms appear 9-90 days after sexual contact. There are 3 main stages:
•Stage 1:
A painless sore appears on the spot where syphilis entered the body. It looks like a small blister or ulcer. The sore will go away in 1-5 weeks without treatment. But you are *still infected.*
•Stage 2:
Starts 4-6 weeks after sexual contact. A rash is all over the body. This rash is very contagious. May also be fever, sore throat (as though you had the flu). Hair might fall out in patches. A highly contagious stage.
The signs will disappear after a few months if not treated.

Complications

Gonorrhea:
If untreated can cause sterility in both men and women, arthritis and disease of prostrate gland (in men).

Syphilis:
•Stage 3:
Happens about two years after sexual contact (can be up to 30 years). Affects about 1/3 of all untreated cases and can cause heart disease, insanity, blindness, deafness, paralysis or death.

How to find out for sure

Gonorrhea:
Consult a doctor for tests:
1) gram stain test
Quick and reliable *if* there are symptoms.
b) culture test
Often used as a back-up test. Discharge is scraped from the penis, vagina, throat, or anus, and treated under special laboratory conditions. Gonorrhea germs can usually be detected if present within 16-48 hours. If gonorrhea is suspected but not proven, then doctor may treat with antibiotics, to be on the safe side.

Syphilis:
Consult doctor for blood test. These are very reliable.

In stage 1, a scraping taken from the sore and examined under a microscope may show the germ. A blood test may not show the presence of syphilis at this stage.

Treatment and follow-up

Gonorrhea:
Penicillin tablets or, more usually, injections. Other anti-biotics are used if you are allergic to penicillin, or if the strain of the disease is resistant to penicillin.
One visit and a follow-up visit a couple weeks later to make sure the germs are killed off.

Syphilis:
Similar treatment. Cure takes about two weeks. Then need blood test once a month for next three months.

irritated by the sometimes vigorous rubbing of heterosexual intercourse. Any continous irritation to the urinary opening, though, can cause this infection.

Symptoms of cystitus are a burning pain when you urinate, and a frequent desire to urinate. It's important to get prompt medical attention when you have cystitus; untreated, it could give you a kidney infection, which is more serious.

When you go to the doctor, your urine will be analyzed and you'll be treated with either sulfa drugs or antibiotics. Black women must be cautious about using sulfa drugs, though — about one American black in eight has an inherited blood deficiency of an enzyme called G6PD. For anyone with this deficiency, the use of sulfa drugs could be fatal. The test for a G6PD deficiency is simple and you should refuse to be treated with sulfa drugs until you have been given this test. Women with a G6PD deficiency are usually treated for cystitus with an antibiotic called ampicillin.

Venereal warts can appear on the sex organs of men or women about three months after sexual contact, or other close physical contact, with someone who is infected.

These warts look ugly, but apart from causing some irritation, they are not harmful.

Perhaps the most important thing about venereal warts is that they may *not* be warts — but the sign of some more serious disease, like syphilis. A blood test is the only sure way to find out.

One or two visits to a doctor is usually enough to clear up the virus that causes venereal warts.

Hepatitis is another disease that can be spread sexually. It's a serious liver disease that gay men need to watch for.

Hepatitis can be caught in many ways — not only by

sexual contact. However, sucking a penis or anus, or kissing, are common ways of picking up hepatitis from someone who has it.

Early signs are like those of the flu — muscle aches and pains, tiredness and fever. These signs usually disappear after some time, and then your urine turns brown and your feces (shit) turns white. Later signs are loss of appetite and jaundice (skin and eyes turn yellow).

The treatment for hepatitis is lots of rest and special diet. There is no permanent cure. The disease may return if you get too tired and run down.

You don't remain infectious, however. Hepatitis can be detected by a blood test, and the doctor will tell you when it is safe to have sex again. This may be some time after the symptoms have all disappeared.

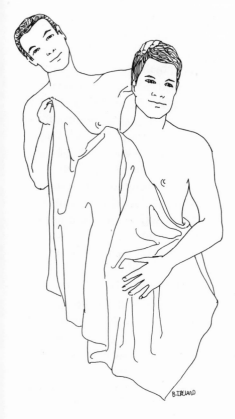

Vaginal infections are a problem women sometimes face. It is part of the body's normal cleansing process to produce a discharge occasionally to clean out the vagina. This discharge is usually clear or white-colored. It may have an odor, but it's not usually strong-smelling.

If you have a discharge that's different from this, or if your vaginal area is itchy, it's a good idea to get some medical attention.

The two main sorts of vaginal infections are candiasis (yeast infection) and trichomoniasis (trich). Both trich and yeast infections can be passed on by sexual contact, or by using a wash cloth, towel, or toilet seat that was used by an infected woman. Yeast infections are most likely brought on by changes in your body (such as pregnancy, diabetes, taking antibiotics, infections, or being under stress). Heterosexual women often get yeast infections from taking birth control pills. Yeast infections are sometimes passed back and forth from a women's mouth to another woman's vagina because a yeast infection can develop in the throat, where it's called thrush.

The two discharges are quite different:
Trich: foul-smelling, clear/ greenish;
Yeast: thick and white, like cottage cheese, a smell like yeast.

You can do a lot to prevent vaginitus. Wearing cotton underpants helps because synthetic cloths (like nylon) hold in the moisture of the vagina, and this gives yeast or other infections a good environment to grow in. Wearing looser pants helps because tight pants also hold the moisture in. You can spread yeast from your anus to your vagina when you wipe yourself after going to the bathroom, so it helps to wipe yourself from front to back instead. Don't share washcloths and towels. Avoid eating too much sugar, or refined foods. Get enough sleep, and enough vitamins B, C, A, and E. If you're run down, or unhealthy, it's easier to get vaginitus.

It also helps to avoid chemicals (harsh soaps, perfumes, commercial douches or sprays). They can upset the natural vaginal environment. Women can have yeast bacteria present in their vaginas without it causing an infection. This is because the yeast is kept in balance by the acids in the vagina. Washing your vagina with regular soap, which is alkaline, can upset the balance between acids and alkalines in the vagina and allow the yeast to multiply. Douching too often also upsets the natural balance, and regular douching is not necessary because the vagina has its own way of cleansing itself. However, special douches can be helpful as a treatment for infections.

Applying cool compresses to the vaginal area, or sitting in a bath, can soothe the itching. Some women have had success with home remedies. Call your local Women's Health Clinic for more specific information and medical advice.

Women should not douche before coming in for a gynecological examination. The treatment for trich is Metronidazole (the brand name is Flagyl). You take Flagyl as pills (in your mouth) 3 times a day for 10 days. During this time you should not have sexual contact with anyone because you could still infect them or be reinfected by your partner.

The treatment for yeast infections is an antibiotic called Nystatin (a brand name is Mycostatin). You take it in the form of vaginal suppositories. You insert the suppositories into the vagina twice a day for ten days, with an applicator, in much the same way you insert a tampon. It works best if you lie down for at least 15 minutes after putting the suppository in because it will melt and leak out soon after you stand up. Putting one in before you go to sleep at night is a good idea.

A word about vaginal deodorants: Women's magazines are full of ads telling you to be clean and sweet-smelling by using ''intimate deodorants.'' It is best to avoid these products. They are unnecessary — your lover will probably find your own smell attractive. They also irritate the inside of the vagina, causing more discharge. If applied just before intercourse they can lead to quite severe burning pain. For cleansing purposes, the best thing is warm water and a mild soap like baby soap.

Herpes (pronounced her-pees) is a virus that is usually passed on during sex. In recent years it has become more common among women.

The signs are groups of painful blisters — like cold sores — appearing on the sex organs or other areas of sexual contact (such as thighs or buttocks). The sores soon break and ooze clear fluid. These open sores can easily become infected. Herpes is very contagious when a person has contact with these sores.

After seven to ten days the blisters go away, but the disease may still be there. You can have relapses for years — especially during times of stress — but the first attack is usually the worst.

There is no known effective treatment for herpes. Most treatments are oriented toward relieving pain and itching, and making the blisters heal faster.

Vitamin E oil directly applied to the sore, B vitamin supplements, comfrey leaf applied directly, and other herbal and nutritional remedies have sometimes been helpful.

A woman who has had a herpes infection has an increased chance of cervical cancer and should have regular pap smears.

Crabs are a type of lice that make their home — by the hundreds — in pubic hair. Occasionally they'll wander onto other hairy parts of the body too. You'll know they are there by the severe itch. Crabs can be passed on by direct contact of infested areas, or contact with infested clothing or blankets.

Each crab is about 1 to 2 millimeters long — less than a tenth of an inch. Their usual color is clear or white, but after a blood meal they turn black or red.

Ordinary soap won't get rid of crabs. You need to treat the infested area with something like Kwell (for which you need a prescription) or any of several non-prescription drugs like Rid (which, however, may be less effective). Follow the instructions that come with the lotion, applying it to all infested areas, but avoid the opening of the penis, the inner vaginal lips and the vaginal opening.

Bedclothes and underwear must be decontaminated at the same time.

Scabies are little mites that burrow unerneath the skin and leave small scabby tracks. They show up in lots of places, especially the wrists, and often on the ankles, near the groin or under the arms. They are very itchy, especially at night.

Scabies are passed on during sex by skin contact, but they can also be picked up from sheets and towels. The treatment is the same as for crabs. If not treated, scabies do no great harm, but they are annoying.

Many doctors have bad attitudes toward homosexuality. They don't like us and they think we're sick in the head.

If your doctor starts giving you this feeling, go to another doctor! Their job is to make you feel better.

Some doctors even make you feel bad about getting V.D. Just remember, V.D. is like any other disease. It's nothing to be ashamed of, just a nuisance until it's cured.

Sometimes it's hard to get the kind of answers you need to understand your body and how to take good care of yourself. Most doctors will assume you are heterosexual and might not tell you what you need to know as a gay person. Especially if you're a woman, and the doctor is a man, he may talk down to you or be impatient when you ask questions. The doctor may think that women are supposed to be quiet and let other people, mostly men, take care of them and do their thinking for them.

The medical profession is dominated by men, and there is still a lot to be learned about women's health. Doctors are not always well informed about women's health, or about gay health. You have a right to know what is happening and to find out how you can take better care of yourself. You have a right to ask questions.

Most gay groups and hotlines

can recommend doctors or clinics that have positive attitudes about homosexuality.

One last thing. Get the proper treatment when you are sick. Pay attention to your body. For certain problems, with proper advice and information, people have had success with home remedies. It's good to learn how to help yourself. But it's important to remember that there are illnesses you don't know about and if you're sick, things can go wrong and you could become sicker. If you're watching your health, you can help a doctor to be more informed about your body.

If you can't afford a doctor, phone your county health department and explain your situation. They should be able to help you find a clinic that's free or affordable.

More letters

Dear friends,

You asked me to write something about coming out. So here is what I remember. I knew I wasn't attracted to girls at about the age of 12 or 13, though certainly I tried hard to deny it to myself at the time. If anyone had suggested I was homosexual, I would have been horrified. But one thing was there. I liked guys. I couldn't change it. I fantasized about men, and imagined all sorts of situations.

A strange thing is that I can never remember not being attracted to them. It seems to have gone on all through. My parents don't fit that dominant-mother/ passive-father cliche usually blamed, so where it came from, I don't know. It was just there. I had to accept it eventually, although it really took until I was almost 16 to understand the full implications of my feelings, of what would happen later, lifestyle, etc. It seems quite a shock to go through thinking of yourself as entirely, well, normal, and in the back of your mind to realize that in one respect you differ.... I guess it's hard for anyone to accept, especially with a Catholic background, and with no outside gay influences, no one and nothing to blame. I wouldn't want anyone to go through the troubles I had, though probably I'm better off for them.

I guess it happens to everyone, discovering themselves. There is so much more than can be written associated with the problem. The feelings when you are turned on by someone you know is "straight," and not being able to talk to them about it. The feelings when you find you talk easily with girls, but there's little attraction. I think loving straights is the hardest part of it. You know it's impossible from the start and still you go on. I had a friend, one of the best looking guys in the school, just as a friend, but a best friend. We did all sorts of things together (but not sexual relations at all) until I decided that I liked him far too much for my and his own good. (He was straight.) He couldn't understand why. I eventually told him what I thought I was. One day we did get it on, but he remains straight to this day. There seem to be people who are mostly heterosexual, but like to "swing the other way" for a while every now and then. I've met others.

One day I learned about a gay disco called The 1270. I finally got up the nerve to go there. When I went in, I had a great weight-removing feeling. This was the gay scene. Something I was totally unfamiliar with. Drag queens, effeminates, as

well as the "ordinary" looking gays — all together in this place. I was stunned and shocked at first.

It's hard to get used to other people's sexual tastes and preferences I guess from where I sit on "the scale." It's hard to see why they like what they like... but now, because I've seen a fair amount of the gay scene to date, I have a much broader picture. It's good now to be able to accept people more. Once, I had a very narrow perception of what a "good" person was. Now I socialize much more easily (to the detriment of studies!).

My friends have helped a lot. A couple living several miles away have really guided me. Not just taken me to the right places, but, just the fact that they are gay, and they have a relationship that works, have had for some time, perhaps helped me find a little stability at a time when I was .experimenting in many other worlds too.

Now, I think I'm happy to be gay. My friends at school know, and there are no problems. I can be open, now. For a long time, I couldn't. They all respect my ideas and personality. It's incredible. Once I wouldn't have believed it.

At one stage I was rushed off to a psychiatrist by worried parents. He just told me not to put a name on myself until I knew for sure. I knew then. I know now. If I ever find myself attracted to a woman, I'll know I'm changing. But at 17, I'm as sure of what I want, as most straights are of what they want.

— Christopher

Dear People,
Hi! My name is Ian... I'm gay. I'm also fifteen, so as you can gather, I go to school...

I realized I was homosexual (or at least I realized I was attracted to men) around the age of 14, in fact it might have been even before that, I'm not sure. It took a little while to understand these feelings. After all, I *was* told homosexuality is/was bad. Actually, whether or not I was told this I'm not sure, the way kids used the words "fag" and "dyke" (although I had a vague idea of the meanings) it just *had* to be bad. Although I had an inkling that I was homosexual, I just couldn't be sure.

One of the things that started me thinking about it was the film *Birds of a Feather*. I was talking about it with some friends and I said I felt sorry for homosexuals because of how they get treated. Everyone — at least the adults — was afraid that I was homosexual, so I explained what I meant. That cleared their minds. I had been Christian on and off for years before I realized I was gay (in fact it was a while after that, that I really felt I was).

I've been called "fairy" for years because of the fact that I don't like sport, bashing other males, acting tough, my features (facial), also, people might have been afraid of my intelligence in lots of ways.... People also think that I've got a feminine voice.

My first sexual experiences happened at a pop festival. Naturally, I enjoyed them. That was the last step in my realization that I was gay. It's quite bad not being able to be "me," instead, I have to act straight.

I have told my father that I'm gay, but I couldn't tell him about my sexual experiences because these men would most likely end up in jail and I would probably end up in an institution because I would be in "moral danger."

Yours in solidarity,
Ian.

More reading

A bibliography compiled by Jearld Moldenhauer and
Siong Huat Chua of Glad Day Bookshop, Boston

Women's fiction

Ruby, by Rosa Guy (Bantam).
A novel about two black
teenage women of different
cultural backgrounds and
temperament, struggling
towards self-identity amidst the
turmoil of the militant black
movement of the 60's and early
70's.

Rubyfruit Jungle, by Rita Mae
Brown (Bamtam).
The adventures of Molly Bolt, a
poor but up-front lesbian from
the deep South who accepts flak
from no one about her
lesbianism. A thoroughly
enjoyable and inspiring book.

Patience & Sarah, by Isabelle
Miller (McGraw-Hill).
Although it's out of print now,
you may find this book in the
library. It's based on a true
story of two young women in
the early nineteenth century
who fall in love.

Desert of the Heart, by Sharon
Isabelle (Talon Books).
The story of a romance between
an older woman and younger
woman, and how they resolve
the conflicts caused by their age
difference. Another good book
by Jane Rule is *The Young in
One Another's Arms*.

Happy Endings Are All Alike,
by Sandra Scoppettone (Dell).
An adolescent lesbian relationship is almost destroyed by a
disturbed straight teenage boy
who threatens the couple with
violence and then blackmail.
But the experience strengthens
the couple's love and raises
their consciousness to the point
where they are prepared to
strike back and declare their
lesbianism openly. Strong in its
portrayal of the many pressures
from families and peers faced
by young lesbians.

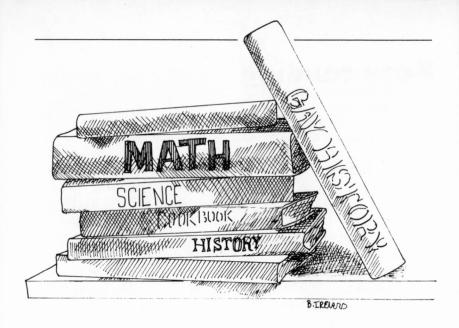

B. IRELAND

Men's fiction

A Candle for St. Anthony, by Eleanor Spence (Oxford University Press).
An Australian schoolboy greets a new kid in school — an Austrian emigrant — with hostility which is quickly transformed into admiration and a friendship which eclipses all his previous pastimes. The story documents his attempt to come to terms with his gay feelings amidst the taunts and destructive peer pressures of his homophobic Australian schoolmates.

I'll Get There, It Better Be Worth the Trip, by John Donovan (Dell).
Two boys, each experiencing the loneliness of a broken home are drawn closer by their need for love and companionship, their friendship culminating in an unforeseen moment of open sexuality. The affirmation of homosexuality at the end of the novel is ambiguous; we are not sure if it is just a phase they are going through.

Trying Hard to Hear You, by Sandra Scoppettone (Bantam). A summer of painful self-discovery for three adolescents, told from the perspective of Camilia, a high school girl who has to confront her attitudes when she learns that two of her closest friends are gay.

Consenting Adults, by Laura Z. Hobson (Warner Books). A useful alternative to the non-fiction books written for parents of gays. A mother describes her emotional reaction to her son's "coming out."

The Persian Boy, by Mary Renault (Bantam). Alexander's young love, Bagoas tells the story of the Conqueror's exploits through Asia Minor. A thoroughly enjoyable, romantic historical novel depicting a period when the homosexual taboo was not. Renault has written several other excellent novels with gay characters, including *The Charioteer*.

The Man Without a Face, by Isabelle Holland (Bantam). A touching story of how a boy gradually discovers his love for an older man, his tutor, only to suppress his affection when he recognizes its homosexual component. A telling tale of how love is destroyed when we recognize the labels we are told to hate.

Sticks and Stones, by Lynn Hall (Dell). Not so much a book about homosexuality as about homophobia, and how it almost destroys the relationship of two young men in a small town. An interesting depiction of how the homosexual taboo operates to ensure that relationships between men do not go beyond the competitive and the uncaring, even when they are non-sexual.

Special Teachers/Special Boys, by Peter Fisher and Marc Rubin (St. Martin's Press). Based on the real life experiences of the authors, this novel takes place in a special

New York City school for adolescents convicted of serious crimes. One of the teachers decides to come out and in so doing brings out a gay student. The 'coming out' stories are realistically depicted: the boy's story is especially interesting in terms of chronicling the new choices available to a city kid with the growth of open gay cultures in our larger cities.

B. IRELAND

Coming out to parents

*A Family Matter: A Parents'
Guide to Homosexuality*, by
Dr. Charles Silverstein
(McGraw-Hill).
A gay psychologist's case-study
approach to counselling
families of gays. Offers parents
the information and guidance
they need to retain their gay
children's love and respect.

*Now That You Know: What
Every Parent Should Know
About Homosexuality*, edited
by Betty Fairchild (Harcourt,
Brace, Jovanovich).
It's probably as hard for your
parents to learn that you're gay
as it is for you to tell them. This
book, written by parents of gay
children, guides parents
through the various emotional,
intellectual and political
challenges they commonly face
on learning of their children's
gayness.

Non-fiction: General

A Way of Love, A Way of Life,
by Frances Hanckel and John
Cunningham (Lothrop, Lee &
Shepard Books).
A very meticulous, "from
square one" guide for young
gays thinking about coming
out. It has chapters designed to
help young people dispel their
anxieties about their sexual
identities, and offers advice on
meeting other gay people and
making contact with the larger
gay community. But the section
on gay sex is sometimes
confusing and anti-sexual.

*With Downcast Gays: Aspects
of Homosexual
Self-Oppression*, by Andrew
Hodges and David Hutter (Pink
Triangle Press).
A unique essay, discussing how,
as members of this anti-sexual,
sexist and homophobic
(anti-gay) society, we gays have
learned to oppress ourselves.
Read it! You'll never be able to
look at your life the same again.

Society and the Healthy Homosexual, by Dr. George Weinberg (Anchor Press/ Doubleday).
This short book was the first to discuss the major problem gay people gay people face — individual and institutional homophobia (fear or hatred of gays). It has a good analysis of why psychiatrists are usually so down on us.

The Gay Report — Lesbians and Gay Men Speak Out About Sexual Experiences and Lifestyles, ed. by Karla Jay and Allen Young (Summit Books).
For the first time in print, lesbians and gay men themselves talk about their sexual experiences away from the self-serving categorization and pigeon-holing definitions of straight sex scientists. Out of 5000 responses to their questionnaires, Jay and Young have compiled this fascinating volume celebrating the truly diverse sexual and social experiences of lesbians and gay men. Jay and Young have written several other excellent books about gay culture and politics.

Word is Out: Stories of Some of Our Lives, by Nancy Adair and Casey Adair (New Glide Publications/A Delta Special).
The full text of the interviews that became the widely praised film documentary. A diverse group of lesbians and gay men of various socio-economic backgrounds, race and age speak about the painful early years of isolation, of oppression and self-oppression, of coming out and in general about their personal-political responses to living in a homophobic, sexist society. There is much to identify with and more to learn from. Shatters lots of stereotypes about gay people.

History

Gay American History, by Jonathan Katz (Avon).
A rich collection of documents covering the 17th century to the 1960's, which retrieves the lost history of the countless gay men and lesbians whose loves and lives have been systematically ignored, distorted and hidden by heterosexual scholarship to maintain the myth of the universality of heterosexuality.

The Early Homosexual Rights Movement [1864-1935], by John Lauritsen and David Thorstad (Times Change Press).
There was a gay liberation movement in Germany at the beginning of this century. It advanced the cause of gay rights — legally, scientifically and culturally — until the 1930's when Stalinist and Nazi repression obliterated all traces of it. This book gives a sense of history to our present movement.

Homosexuality: A History From Ancient Greece to Gay Liberation, by Vern Bullough (New American Library).
Includes chapters about lesbianism, homosexuality in the schools, gender roles, and the effect of religion in forming our attitudes. This book makes an excellent introductory reading in gay history.

Non-fiction: Men

The New Gay Liberation Book: Writings and Photographs on Gay [Men's] Liberation, edited by Len Richmond and Gary Noguera (Ramparts Press).
A rich collection of both personal reflections and analytical essays. Includes contributions on the anti-Anita Bryant campaign and the politics surrounding the election and murder of Harvey Milk. Contributors include John Rechy, Paul Goodman, Christopher Isherwood and Tom Robinson.

Men Loving Men: A Gay Sex Guide and Consciousness Raising Book, by Mitch Walker (Gay Sunshine Press).
The sex techniques are probably nothing new except to the sexually naive but the positive and direct approach taken by this book to gay male sexuality is fresh and liberating, especially if you are just coming out and still have some of those old closet hangups.

Familiar Faces, Hidden Lives, by Howard Brown, M.D. (Harcourt, Brace, Jovanovich). The author explores the many facets of gay life in various parts of the US, both large cities and small towns.

Unbecoming Men (Times Change Press).
A group of seven men record their consciousness-raising attempts to "unbecome men." In their words, they attempt "to trace our experiences back to their roots, discovering how we learned to be male and sexist, to oppress women and dehumanize ourselves — how we became 'men.' "

Non-fiction: Women

Our Right to Love: A Lesbian Resource Book, edited by Ginny Vida (Prentice Hall). This bright, joyful, well-illustrated guide has essays on every aspect of lesbianism including relationships, sexuality, activism, legal matters and culture.

The Lesbian Primer, by Liz Diamond (Women's Educational Media, Inc.) This very basic book about lesbianism is designed to dispel some myths and to promote an understanding of lesbian lifestyles. It's helpful for both heterosexuals and gays who haven't had much contact with lesbianism.

Lesbian Lives: Biographies of Women From the Ladder, edited by Barbara Grier and Coletta Reid (Diana Press). A valuable collection of brief biographies and photos of famous lesbians. Will serve as a basic resource and impetus for further research and reading in lesbian herstory.

Amazon Expedition (Times Change Press).
A collection of 10 essays that combine lesbian politics and feminism.

The Joy of Lesbian Sex, by Dr. Emily Sisley and Bertha Harris (Simon & Schuster).
An attractive and forthright volume showing by words and pictures, all aspects of lesbian lovemaking plus "everything a woman needs to know in order to survive as a lesbian in a straight world."

A Woman's Touch: An Anthology of Lesbian Eroticism and Sensuality For Women Only, edited by Cedar and Nelly (Womanshare Books).
Fourteen stories and one essay explore very diverse visions and tales of lesbian sexuality and eroticism.

B.IRELAND

Getting in touch

A lot of times in this book we've mentioned getting in touch with gay organizations in your area. That's fine if you know of such organizations. If you don't, here are some suggestions for finding out about them:

• Check the phone book under the word "Gay". There may be a Gay Hotline or Gay Alliance or similar group listed.
• If there's nothing in your city, try the nearest larger town. Although a group there may be too far away to be of much immediate value to you, they should know what's going on closer to you. Once you've explained your situation, you'll probably find them eager to help out.
• If there's any type of women's center or feminist group in town, they'll probably know of gay activities that are going on. Give them a call.

Once you've made friends with a few gays in your area, you'll find it's much easier to meet others, and to find out about gay dances, marches, bars, and whatever else you'd like to know about.

Put this book where it belongs

In publishing a book like this, we face a big problem: we know that this is an important and unique book for young people who are beginning to think about their sexuality, or to recognize their gayness — and yet it's difficult to get a book like this into places where those young people can read it.

Many of you reading this will be in a position to help. Here's what you can do:

• Ask your local library to order this book, and give them our address (on the last page). Many libraries will order virtually any book that is requested.

• If you're a teacher, ask your school library to also order it.

• If you work in a youth center, make *Young, Gay and Proud!* available there. You can use the bulk rates on the last page to get extra copies to give away or to sell.

Other books from Alyson Publications

Reflections of a Rock Lobster: $4.95
A story about growing up gay
by Aaron Fricke

Guess who's coming to the prom! No one in Cumberland, Rhode Island, was surprised when Aaron Fricke appeared at his high school prom with a male date. He had sued his school for the right to do so, and the media had been full of the news.

Yet for the first sixteen years of his life, Fricke had closely guarded the secret of his homosexuality. *Reflections of a Rock Lobster* is his story about growing up with this secret. With insight and humor, Fricke tells how he first became aware of his homosexual feelings in childhood, then learned to hide them from adults, and then to repress his feelings completely, before he finally developed a positive gay identity. '*Rock Lobster* is simply the most realistic, revealing, painful, insightful and — finally — joyful story about growing up gay in America that you will ever read.' (John Preston in *New York Native*.)

The Men With the Pink Triangle* $4.95
by Heinz Heger

For decades, historians have ignored the persecution of homosexuals by the Nazi regime. Now a man who survived six years in the Nazi concentration camps has finally told about that terrible era. **The Men With the Pink Triangle** is the intensely personal story of a young Austrian student who was abruptly arrested by the Gestapo in 1939 for being homosexual. He spent the next six years in German concentration camps; like other homosexual prisoners, he was forced to wear a pink triangle on his shirt so he could be readily identified for special mistreatment. His story is often depressing, but it is one you will never forget. 'One of the Ten Best Books of the Year' (Richard Hall, *The Advocate*).

The Incredible Shrinking American Dream $6.95
by Estelle Carol, Rhoda Grossman and Bob Simpson

History should have been this much fun in high school! The authors have written a comic-book history of the US that will entertain you while it brings to light the often-forgotten history of working people, women and minorities. 'Terrific! A solid class analysis of the American past, in words and pictures that are a delight to the eye and to the funny bone' (Bertell Ollman, creator of the *Class Struggle* game).

Beyond the Fragments: $6.95
Feminism and the making of socialism
by Sheila Rowbotham, Lynne Segal and Hilary Wainwright
   Three women who have been active in both feminist and socialist politics examine the implications of the women's movement on leftist politics. They argue not just for a rhetorical acceptance of feminism, but for a redefinition of priorities, a new approach to theory and consciousness, and for an open and searching examination of past and present forms of political organization. (Publication date: October 1981. Orders received earlier will be shipped immediately upon publication.)

The Spiral Path: A gay contribution to human survival* $6.95
by David Fernbach
   What does gay liberation have to do with environmental pollution or the threat of nuclear war? How can gay people help bring the present crisis of humanity to an outcome of survival and higher evolution? These are the bold questions tackled in *The Spiral Path*, a discussion that ranges from genetic engineering to the origins of male supremacy. The author integrates gay liberation, feminism and socialism with a rich experience in progressive politics. *The Spiral Path* is serious without being academic; it combines theoretical debate with personal testimony, and explores many questions that have long been ignored by the left.

Pink Triangles: Radical perspectives on gay liberation $4.95
ed. by Pam Mitchell
   The American left and the gay movement have a great deal to offer each other. The essays in this book give new insights, from a progressive viewpoint, on such subjects as pornography, pedophilia, community building, and theories of gay liberation.

*Published separately in Great Britain by Gay Men's Press, 27 Priory Ave., London, N8 7RN, England.

Coming Out in the Seventies $5.95
by Dennis Altman

Is the gay movement being coopted by Madison Avenue? How would E.M. Forster's writings have changed, had he been open about his homosexuality? What mechanisms does the state use to control society's sexual norms? These are but a few of the questions that Dennis Altman raises in his new book.

Energy, Jobs and the Economy $3.45
by Richard Grossman and Gail Daneker

Sure you're in favor of solar energy. But what about your Uncle Joe, who's worried that without nuclear power we'll have blackouts and plant closings and that he may lose his job? This highly readable book shows that solar and renewable energy sources are not only safer than nuclear power, they're also better for the economy and for working people.

Ask for these titles in your bookstore. If unavailable locally, you may order them directly from Alyson Publications, Dept. B7, PO Box 2783, Boston, MA 02208. Please enclose full payment with your order and add 75¢ postage on orders for one book. (If you order two or more books, we'll pay postage.)

To order this book in bulk:

To make *Young, Gay and Proud!* more widely available, we're offering the following reduced prices when you buy more than one copy. Please include payment with your order, as shown below. These prices are post-paid; add $1.00 for rush orders. Outside the U.S., add $.15 per book.

2 or 3 copies: $2.75 each
4 to 9 copies: $2.50 each
10 to 19 copies: $2.00 each
20 to 59 copies: $1.75 each
60 or more copies: $1.40 each

Send your orders to the address above.